YOUR KNOWLEDGE HAS VALUE

Bibliographic information published by the German National Library:

The German National Library lists this publication in the National Bibliography; detailed bibliographic data are available on the Internet at http://dnb.dnb.de .

Imprint:

Copyright © 2016 GRIN Verlag, Open Publishing GmbH
Print and binding: Books on Demand GmbH, Norderstedt Germany
ISBN: 9783656989325

This book at GRIN:

http://www.grin.com/en/e-book/335004/shangwe-rainmaking-ceremonies-from-a-functionalist-perspective

Norman Mberengwa

Shangwe rainmaking ceremonies from a functionalist perspective

GRIN Publishing

GRIN - Your knowledge has value

Since its foundation in 1998, GRIN has specialized in publishing academic texts by students, college teachers and other academics as e-book and printed book. The website www.grin.com is an ideal platform for presenting term papers, final papers, scientific essays, dissertations and specialist books.

Visit us on the internet:

http://www.grin.com/

http://www.facebook.com/grincom

http://www.twitter.com/grin_com

THE SHANGWE RAINMAKING CEREMONIES FROM A FUNCTIONALIST PERSPECTIVE

BY NORMAN MBERENGWA

(B.A Theology and religious Studies, Midlands State university, Zimbabwe)

KEY TERMS : Functionalist approach, Rainmaking ceremonies, Shangwe

TABLE OF CONTENTS

ABSTRACT

The Shangwe rainmaking ceremonies can be approached from different perspectives. Each perspective is subjective to the researcher's background or theological motif. The ceremonies however declined in 2004 when the last rainmaker and spirit medium, Nevana Tavasiira Marariromba died in 2004 and the spirit failed to choose a successor up to this time of writing. The functionalist perspective to the Shangwe rain making ceremony is based on an exploration of the functions that the rain making ceremony provided to the Shangwe people. This article explores ten functions that the Shangwe rainmaking ceremonies provided to the Shangwe people.

BACKGROUND TO THE STUDY

Rainmaking ceremonies, in the past, were mostly practised in many parts of Africa. Despite the fact that some parts of Africa no longer take rainmaking ceremonies into serious considerations, it is possible that some conservative Africans still consider this ceremony as essential in their expression of religiosity. In some cases, these conservative Africans attempt to re-establish their precious tradition but fail due to various circumstances. According to Mbiti (1970:225) "Rainmakers are another useful and important category of specialist found in many parts of Africa." Rainmakers were important like most African Traditional Religious sacred practioners because of their role of consulting the deity through rituals which would invoke the deity to provide rains. This link between rainmakers and the deity made the office of a rainmaker a necessity in almost all parts of Africa especially during the time of drought.

There are various Shona terms used to refer to the rainmaking ceremony. Matsuhira (2013:169) states that in Shona terminology, the rainmaking ceremony is called *"bira rekukumbira mvura"*, *"mukwerera"* or*"rukuruva."* In most cases, the rainmaking ceremony is celebrated at the beginning of the rain season. The celebration of the rainmaking ceremony is crucial in African Traditional Religion is important because it is a sign of showing allegiance to the of provider of rain.

The Shangwe rain making ceremony was practiced at Nevana Shrine which is located under chief Chireya. The Shrine is still existing but the ceremonies are no longer done due to various factors of which the most of these factors is the death of the last Nevana, Tavasiira Marariromba who died in 2004.(Ngara,2014).

AN UNDERSTANDING OF THE SHANGWE PEOPLE

The Shangwe people are the original inhabitants of Gokwe District. This district is found in the Midlands Province of Zimbabwe. From the Shangwe oral tradition, the term *Shangwe* was derived from a mountain. However, according to Nyambara(2002) the term Shangwe was used by the Madheruka immigrants to refer to the state of primitivism and backwardness of the original inhabitants of Gokwe. The Shangwe people themselves deny this negative meaning attached to the term *Shangwe*. They argue that since the term *Shangwe* was derived from a mountain, it therefore refers to a place rather than the state of people.

Maravanyika (2012) highlights that *Madheruka* is a term first used to refer to all migrants who came to Gokwe from various areas around the 1960s . Maravanyika(2012) notes that the Madheruka people came from various areas like Mberengwa, Gutu, Bikita, Mwenezi Churumhanzu and many other areas.

Beach(1994) assets that the Shangwe, like any other Shona clans came from Guruuswa and they established a *Shava* (eland totem) confederacy which was led by the paramount chief Chireya.

FUNCTIONALIST PERSPECTIVE ON THE SHANGWE RAINMAKING CEREMONIES

The French sociologist, Emile Durkheim (1858-1917) provides an understanding of religion from a functionalist perspective. Durkheim (1912) notes that religion is eminently social and provides social solidarity and a meaning for life. The functionalist perspective on the Shangwe rain making ceremony focus on the functions that the ceremony provided to the Shangwe people. These include the sociological, political, economic, cosmological, numinological, pneumatological, ethical, psychological, philosophical and ritual functions

The sociological functions

Cox (2010;6) notes that "religion is a cooperative quest for a satisfying life." This kind of cooperation to attain a satisfying life was exhibited by the Shangwe people during rain making ceremonies at Nevana Shrine. Cox further goes on to supports his view by quoting the South African scholar, Martin Prozesky (1984;153) who views religion as a quest for ultimate well-being. Considering the Shangwe rain making ceremony, several people from all the Shangwe chiefdoms such as the paramount chief Chireya, the sub-chiefs such as Nemangwe, Sai, Mukoka and Njelele went on an annual pilgrimage to the Shangwe shrine at

Nevana for a common cause; a request for the rains. (VaTasara interviewee, 28 May 2016). The rainmaking ceremony promoted social interaction and unity as the Shangwe people unanimously and committedly showed their total dependence to Mwari, their deity whose powers are decentralised. Being by Nevana, the spirit medium and sacred practioners who were assistants to Nevana, the Shangwe rainmaking ceremony facilitated regional integration through co-operative efforts to solve their common problem. Cooperation was not an option, but a prerequisite since rituals had to be followed precisely, lack of cooperation would lead to wrong procedures which would lead to wrong results. (Chiremba, interviewee, 28 May 2016).Thus it can be argued that the rain making ceremony promoted social functions such as solidarity, unity, cooperation and value consensus.

The political functions

In many parts of Africa, rainmakers are involved in political affairs. The Shona spirit mediums, Nehanda and Kaguvi participated in the First Chimurenga. Mbiti(1970;225) gives another example of the Luvedu Rain Queen who was the head of the nation and the symbol of its welfare. According to him,the rainmaker 's function was not only to make rain, but could also stop rains to fall on the land of his enemies. In the context of the Shangwe rain making ceremony, it can be noted that the rainmaker 's function was not confined to the religious spheres,but participated in the political spheres since the dichotomy between religion and politics is untenable in the Shangwe worldview(personal observations). The rainmaker, Nevana Tavasiira Marariromba,by virtue of him being closer to the tribal spirit, and above all,being a tribal spirit medium(svikiro) could receive information about political crisis to befall upon the Shangwe people and lead a ritual procession to resolve that political crisis. In most cases, the rainmaker also intervened in the political disputes such as succession disputes among the Shangwe chieftainship. Above all, the rainmaking ceremonies ensured that justice had to prevail within the political sphere, Otherwise a ruthless chief, headmen or kraal head who oppress the poor would anger the tribal spirit which in turn would punish the whole Shangwe clan.(Thaddeus Marariromba, interviewee 27 May 2016). Thus the rainmaking ceremony functioned as a pretext for justice in the Shangwe political dimension.

Economic functions

The Shangwe rain making ceremonies acted as buffers that resisted drought.Drought was the most feared enemy that would jeopardise the Shangwe health and well-being. In most cases such as the 1992 drought in Zimbabwe, the Shangwe lost most of their livestock and the crops deteriorated to such an extent that the Shangwe had to rely on their traditional foodstuffs which consists of *manyenya* and *svosvi*. Manyenya are wild tubers similar to sweet potatoes. They are boiled and eaten. Svozvi are wild pea-like fruits that are boiled for at least a week in an open fire before they can be eaten. Maravanyika (2014;3) notes that the Shangwe traditional ceremonies were practiced before the commencement of every economic activity. These activities include farming, hunting and gathering. The fact that rain making ceremonies were done at the beginning of the farming season shows that the ceremony linked the Shangwe deity with the economic affairs of the clan. Therefore, the Shangwe rainmaking ceremony functioned as a web of the clan's networks.

Cosmological functions

The term cosmos is derived from the Medieval Latin word *cosmologia* and from the Greek word *kosmos*. The Advanced English Dictionary defines cosmology, (*cosmogony or cosmogeny*) as the study of the evolution and structure or nature of the universe. Eliade (1957) highlights that space is not homogeneous for a religious man, but interruptions break it into sacred and profane spaces. Eliade (1957) goes on to say that it is only when the sacred manifests in a hierophany for the purpose of revelation of an absolute reality that the homogeneity of space is broken. Cox (1992) notes that mountains are the meeting places between the sacred and profane, for example Matopo Hill is an example where the sacred manifest themselves in a hierophany. Mbiti (1991) notes that African cosmology is expressed in proverbs, myths legends ,wise sayings, rituals and symbols. Aschwanden (1989) and Cox (1992) assert that cosmogonic myths are common among the Shona people. Magesa (1997) defines myths as a language that tries to explain the truth about human existence in a rational way. However, the cosmos is understood from an anthropomorphic sense.

Durkheim(1912) assets that objects that are sacred are such objects which are considered as part and parcel of the spiritual realms. These include objects of reverence, or rites . Profane are such things without religious meaning or function. Durkheim goes on to say that while not undermining the dichotomy between the sacred and profane, it must be taken into cognisance that these two realms depend on each other and interact for survival. The sacred cannot survive without the profane and vice versa.

Considering the Shangwe rainmaking ceremonies, one can note that they were essential in the understanding of the Shangwe cosmological worldview. Firstly, the shrine on which the ceremony was celebrated was considered sacred, an axis mundi and a ladder to the spiritual world. Secondly, the rainmaking ceremony facilitated the Shangwe people with their understanding of cosmogonic myths, for example ,that rains do not fall on a full moon. Thirdly, the ceremony gave the Shangwe people an understanding of the use of hierophanes such as the stick and the *ndiro* (plate), the object of reverence which symbolised procreation. Fourthly, the Shangwe rain making ceremony gave the Shangwe people an understanding that space is not homogeneous, but dichotomised into sacred and profane places. Thus the Nevana Dumba,which is located at the centre of Nevana homestead is sacred while other houses are profane(personal observations). Generally, the rainmaking ceremony acted as a panacea in promoting an understanding of the Shangwe cosmological worldview, both consciously and unconsciously.

An understanding of the numinous (numinological functions)

Rudolf Otto Otto (1917) 's conception of the numinous in not untenable considering how the rainmaking ceremony shaped the Shangwe numinological worldview. To understand how the Shangwe rainmaking ceremony facilitates the numinological understanding of the Shangwe people, we need to examine Rudolf Otto's conception of the numinous.

Otto (1917) describes the numinous as the "*mysterium tremendum et fascinans*" (fearful and fascinating mystery*) "Mysterium*" means that the numinous is "Wholly Other" and experienced with blank wonder and stupor. "Tremendum" (tremendous) means awfulness, terror, demonic dread, awe, absolute unapproachability, *"Fascinans*" (fascinating) refers to the potent charm, and attractiveness in spite of fear or terror.

Considering how the Shangwe rainmaking ceremony promoted an understanding of the numinous, one can note the following facts. Firstly, the numinous is mysterious, fearful but fascinating. Examining the Shangwe rain making ceremonies, one can note that the Shangwe people approached their deity fearfully, with all their respect and following all the rituals. The fear is rooted on an axiomatic supposition that in the event that the rituals are not followed correctly, incorrect results which may include a punishment may befall on the people (Mahohoma, interviewee, 29 May 2016). However, despite the fear of breaking taboos, the Shangwe celebrate in excitement. So generally, the Shangwe rainmaking ceremony is celebrated with excitement mixed with fear and the curiosity of seeing rainfall that is mixed with the fear of not receiving it due to either failure to comply with the taboos or due to breaking of ethical and moral codes of the clan in general. It is a juxtaposition of bitter-sweetness feelings. Thus, considering the feelings that the participants of the Shangwe rainmaking ceremonies experienced, it is plausible to say that ceremony did not only facilitated an understanding of the numinous, but a feeling of the presence of the numinous especially when the tribal spirit was possessed an enter into an ecstatic trance, suspending his volitions and utter a growling sound of the lion as a signal for the arrival (kusvika) of the tribal ancestor, the lion (mhondoro) (Thaddeus Marariromba,interviee,28 May 2016).

Pneumatological functions

The Advanced English Dictionary defines pneumatology as the study of interaction between humans and spiritual beings. Anderson (2003) on his research on African Initiated Churches highlights that pneumatology is highly emphasized in these churches these churches. Pneumatology is not confined to Christianity, but can also be found in African Traditional Religion as evidenced by the Shangwe rainmaking ceremonies. During these ceremonies a relationship based on anticipation and appreciation could be noted: the Shangwe paid ritual offerings in anticipation of rains and the spirit reciprocated by offering rains as an appreciation of rituals. Thus through the rain making ceremonies when the Shangwe expressed their faith in their tribal spirit, they fulfil E.B Taylor's definition of religion: "religion is a belief in spiritual beings." Generally, the rain making ceremonies functioned as a facilitating process in the promotion of the Shangwe pneumatology.

The ethical functions

Ethics were essential in the Shangwe rainmaking ceremonies. From the Shangwe oral tradition, for the rainmaking ceremony to be successful, the Shangwe had to make sure that all ethical and moral standards were followed on their day to day activities. This means that if anyone had broken the ethical standards, the tribal spirit would be angered and punish the whole clan for not abiding with the ethical considerations. Therefore, it can be noted that the ceremony promoted the upholding of moral standards in fear of punishment in the event that the ethics were violated.

Psychological functions

Friedrich Schleiermacher quoted in Cox (2010:5) notes that religion is a feeling of absolute dependence. Cox also takes into account Sigmund Freud psychological explanation of the functions of religion which states that religion provides human beings with comfort and consolation. Considering the Shangwe rainmaking ceremonies, one can note that to this ceremonies were a solution in times of crises. The rainmaker would not only provide a solution to the problem, but find the source of the problem and ask for the right solution to the problem. A ritual was usually offered to the *mhondoro* as a petition for the tribal spirit to revoke the punishment. The Shagwe would sigh with relief if the ritual was accepted. Thus, rituals had much positive input in the Shangwe people's psychological dimension.

The philosophical functions

Feuerbach 's projectionist theory is useful in understanding the philosophical function of the Shangwe rainmaking ceremonies. Feuerbach as quoted in Cox(2010) notes that religion is a human projection to an imaginary being. In the context of the Shangwe rainmaking ceremonies, from a philosophical perspective, it can be noted that the ceremonies promoted human perfection in an anticipation that the imaginary deity demands human perfection. Moreover, the Shangwe rainmaking ceremonies promoted *transference* as in a client-counsellor relationship during crisis counselling. This transference help the client to empty the burden from his mind to the counsellor's mind who then asses the problem and in return, the counsellor gives a solution to the client's problem. Philosophically, the Shangwe rainmaking ceremonies justified the Shangwe people 's helplessness to the problem of droughts as the ceremonies were an indication that they were not responsible for the rains, but the tribal ancestor's responsibility.

Ritual functions

The Shangwe rain making ceremonies promoted rituals among the people. Rituals were important because they acted as an expression of allegiance to the Shangwe deity,Mwari. They promoted a constant interaction between the spiritual and religious worlds. Ngara(2014) notes that before the Shangwe rainmaking ceremonies were done, the Shangwe people offered rituals of purifications so as to approach the deity blameless. Rituals promoted a life of purity.

AN EVALUATION OF FUNCTIONALIST APPROACH TO THE SHANGWE RAINMAKING CEREMONIES

1. The functionalist approach gives a blind eye to the negative part of the Shangwe rainmaking ceremonies

The model assumes that the Shangwe rainmaking ceremonies bring positive functions to the society. This is an overgeneralisation because religion is a double edged sword. In some cases, it promotes antagonism especially when conflicting ideas arise. This is the same scenario the the Shangwe rainmaking ceremonies posed following the aftermaths of the Madheruka people and the establishment of Christianity. The Madheruka people condemned the Shangwe rainmaking ceremonies as outdated and primitive. Nyambara (2002) captures the Madheruka 's attack on the Shangwe status and religious practises. Moreover the Shangwe chiefs tried to enforce this practice to the Madheruka people thus worsening the conflicts.

2. The model ignores how the ceremonies subjugated women

The model also ignores the effects that the practice has to women in the society. In the case of the Shangwe rain making ceremonies, women are subjugated during the dancing ceremonies because they danced with men who are not necessarily their husbands, obliged women to use vulgar words in songs, perform a symbolic sexual enactment and (Ngara,2014) Moreover, young virgins were pledged to the rainmaker as a way of appreciating his duties.

3. The model cannot give a description of how the ceremony was practiced.

The fact that the functinalist approach to the Shangwe rainmaking ceremonies focus on the functions that the ceremony promotes leads the model to ignore a description of how it was practiced. In most cases when the approach gives a description, the motive behind is not to give what actually transpired, but to draw a conclusion to the fuction that such a description given had to the society. It goes straight to the finest detail that promotes a function ,avoiding other issues which it fails to draw a conclusion towards a function. Therefore, the functionalist approach to the Shangwe rain making ceremony promotes reductionism.

4. *The model lacks location, space and time associated with the Shangwe rainmaking ceremony.*

The Shangwe rainmaking ceremonies were not ahistorical events located out of space and time. They were done at a particular geographical location and at a particular time frame. They have an origin and the factors that led to their rise. These ceremonies also have a decline that is attributed to various factors, both long term and immediate factors. However, the model simply focus on the functions but cannot even shade light to the people on whether or not they are still being practiced. If not, the functionalist model does not focus look at the period when they stopped and what caused their decline.

5 The model does not examines who is giving the judgement.

Since the model focuses on the positive functions, it does not pose these questions: Who is outlining the functions? These functions are positive to who? It looks to a society as homogeneous and having the same worldview. In a multi-cultural society, the functionalist approach infringes the rights of the minority by evaluation religion from the shoes of the dominant culture.

CONCLUSIONS

The article concludes that the functionalist approach is essential in outlining the funtions that it brought to the Shangwe society. However, this approach to the phenomena cannot give a holistic understanding of the Shangwe rainmaking ceremonies. The model promotes reductionism. Moreover,it does not give the location, space, time and the negative impact the Shangwe rainmaking ceremonies had on women.

REFERENCES

Beach, D. N, (1980) The Shona and Zimbabwe 900-1850: An Outline of Shona History, Gweru: Mambo Press.

Cox.J.L (2010) An introduction to the phenomenology of religion, London: Continuum.

Durkheim, E.(1912) The Elementary Forms of Religious Life,(Translated byJ.W.Swain) London: Allen and Unwin.

Eliade, M. (1959) The Sacred and the Profane, New York: Harcourt

Freud, S. (1963) Psychoanalysis and faith: the letters of Sigmund Freud & Oskar : New York: Basic Books

Maravanyika S(2012) Local Responses to Colonial Evictions, Conservation and Commodity Policies among Shangwe Communities in Gokwe, North-western Zimbabwe, 1963-1980 African Nebula, Issue 5.

Mbiti.J.S (1970) The Concepts of God in Africa,London:SPCK

Ngara.R(2014) Jichi Dance Structure, Gender and Sexualit, University of Fort Hare.

Nyambara,P.S (2002) "Madheruka and Shangwe: Ethnic Identities and the Culture of Modernity in Gokwe, north-western Zimbabwe, 1963-79, Journal of African History.
Otto ,R (1917) The Idea of the Holy, Oxford: Oxford University.

Norman Mberengwa is an outgoing Theology and Religious Studies student and Midlands State University. He hails from Gokwe area and was once a relief teacher at Nevana Primary School where he became a friend and co-worker of Thaddeus, one of the sons of the late Shngwe rainmaker, Nevana Tvasiira Marariromba. This article is the first step into his field of research.